A common loon preparing to fly

Loons

Jill Kalz

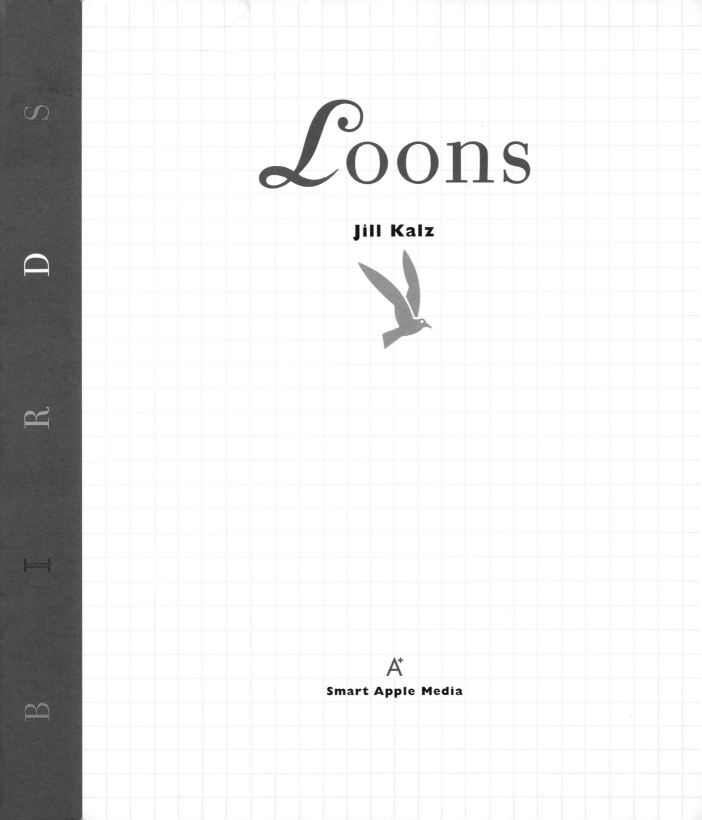

A⁺
Smart Apple Media

COPYRIGHT

Published by Smart Apple Media

1980 Lookout Drive, North Mankato, MN 56003

Designed by Rita Marshall

Copyright © 2003 Smart Apple Media. International copyright reserved in all countries. No part of this book may be reproduced in any form without written permission from the publisher.

Printed in the United States of America

Photographs by Gunter Marx Photography, Gregory M. Nelson, Root Resources (Alan G. Nelson)

Library of Congress Cataloging-in-Publication Data

Kalz, Jill. Loons / by Jill Kalz. p. cm. – (Birds)

Summary: An introduction to the loon, describing how they look, their mating habits, threats to their existence, and more.

ISBN 1-58340-133-4

1. Loon–Juvenile literature. [1. Loon.] I. Title.

QL696.G33 K36 2002   598.4'42–dc21   2001049643

First Edition 9 8 7 6 5 4 3 2 1

Loons

Ancient and Mysterious

The cry of the loon has been called sad, beautiful, and mysterious. It signals the start of spring on northern lakes. It welcomes people back to their summer cabins and fishing boats. And it has been filling the air since the time of the dinosaurs. Loons are among the oldest birds in the world. Scientists have discovered loon-like **fossils** that are more than 65 million years old! Some ancient cultures believed that the loon followed souls to heaven. Others believed that the loon's call signaled rain. Five different kinds, or species, of loons

exist today. They live on lakes, oceans, or rivers in northern

parts of the world. All five species can be found in North

America. The common loon is the best-known species.

Loons spend most of their lives in water

Loon Details

Loons are about the size of geese. They weigh an average of eight pounds (3.6 kg), with a **wingspan** of four feet (1.2 m). All loons are brownish-gray and white in the winter. But in the spring, each species changes color. The common loon, for example, wears a summer "necklace" of white stripes around its black neck and patches of bright white squares on its back. Loons hunt, eat, and sleep on the water. Their strong webbed feet are

Because loons are clumsy on land, their name may have come from the old Scandinavian word *lom,* meaning "clumsy person."

set far back on their bodies. This helps them swim quickly and

gracefully but makes walking on land awkward. 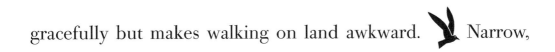 Narrow,

pointed wings help loons steer while swimming and diving. A

Swimming comes naturally to loons

Loon feathers are brightest in the summer

loon's wings and body are covered with rough feathers. Water

slides off these feathers like rain on a waxed car. Soft, velvety

feathers cover the loon's head and neck. Bird bones are

usually hollow, but most of the loon's bones **Baby loons**

are solid. This weight helps the loon dive **can dive a**

foot (30 cm)

underwater

deep into the water for food—as deep as 200 **just two**

days after

feet (61 m)! Loons love fish, especially perch **hatching.**

and catfish. They will also eat frogs, shellfish, and insects.

They use their keen red eyes and long, sharp bills to spot

A loon with a freshly caught crayfish

and catch **prey**. Heavy bones make diving easier, but they make getting up into the air more difficult. Some loons may flap their wings and hop across the water a distance equal to four football fields before they take off. But once they are in the air, they can fly 100 miles (161 km) per hour.

Little Swimmers

In the fall, just before lakes and rivers ice over, loons **migrate**. Most spend their winters near the Atlantic or Pacific coasts. When they return in the spring, loons look for mates.

When in danger, loons rise up and kick

During **courtship**, pairs swim together, side by side, with their bills pointing up toward the sky. Males "yodel" and make quite a bit of noise. Loon calls can sound like crazy laughter, a hoot, a wolf's howl, or even a scream. Each call has a special purpose. It may signal danger, welcome other loons, or warn enemies to stay away. Once

Most loons mate for life; this means a male and female stay together until one of them dies.

they have mated, the male and female loon build a nest together. Loons prefer to build on islands, but they also build

Loon calls can be heard from miles away

nests atop muskrat houses and clumps of reeds close to shore. Nests are made of twigs, grasses, and mud. The female loon usually lays two eggs the size of pears. After about a month, the eggs hatch. Just three hours after hatching, chicks are out on the water atop a parent's back. With good care from their parents, chicks are ready to fly in 10 to 12 weeks.

Survival Threats

A loon in the wild may live 20 years or more. But there are many dangers along the way. Eggs may be eaten by raccoons, skunks, or birds such as gulls. Baby loons may be

snatched by large fish. The loon's biggest threat, however, is

people. Water and air pollution kill the fish that loons need to

survive. Nearly 400 loons were killed by an oil spill off the

Baby loons riding atop their parent's back

coast of Alaska in 1989. Careless boaters and curious swimmers may disturb the loons' nesting sites. This often causes the birds to abandon their eggs. Loons have lived through it all: floods, droughts, the ice age, and the arrival of human beings. If we reduce pollution and provide loons with safe places to nest, their musical cries will fill the air for many years to come.

Baby loons have huge appetites; they may be fed more than 70 times per day during their first week of life.

A nest of loon eggs

Do You Remember?

Loons often migrate great distances yet still find their way back to the same nesting spot each spring. Play this game with your friends to test your "loon memory."

What You Need

Two 8-1/2-inch by 11-inch (22 cm x 28 cm) sheets of heavy paper

A scissors

Crayons

What You Do

1. Fold each sheet of paper in half from top to bottom. Fold it again the same way. Now, fold it from right to left.
2. Open the sheets and cut along the fold lines. You should have a total of 16 "cards."
3. On two cards, draw a nest. Try to make them look exactly alike. On the other seven pairs, draw matching loons, fish, eggs, lakes, chicks, feathers, and boats.
4. Shuffle the cards and lay them face-down in four rows.
5. Taking turns, flip two cards over. Do they match? If not, turn them back over. If they do, try to find another match.

A loon waiting for its eggs to hatch

Index

Words to Know

courtship (KORT-ship)—the time before mating during which a male and female loon get to know each other

fossils (FAH-sullz)—ancient plant or animal remains, such as a skeleton

migrate (MY-grate)—to move from one area to another according to the changing seasons

prey (PRAY)—an animal hunted for food

wingspan (WING-span)—the length from the tip of one outstretched wing to the other

Read More

Klein, Tom. *Loon Magic for Kids*. Minnetonka, Minn.: Creative Publishing International, 1991.

Merrick, Patrick. *Loons (Naturebooks)*. Chanhassen, Minn.: The Child's World, 1999.

Ring, Elizabeth. *Loon at Northwood Lake*. Norwalk, Conn.: Soundprints, 1997.

Internet Sites

About.com, Inc.: Birding/Wild Birds
http://birding.about.com/hobbies/
birding

Kid Info: Birds
http://www.kidinfo.com/science/
birds.html

eNature.com
http://www.eNature.com/guides/
select_birds.asp